Tye Finds A New Home

Kate Dobrowolska

© Kate Dobrowolska 2019

Published by Kate Dobrowolska

Photography: Paul Fowlie

Publishing partner: Paragon Publishing, Rothersthorpe

The rights of Kate Dobrowolska to be identified as the author of this work have been asserted by her in accordance with the Copyright, Designs and Patents Act of 1988.

All rights reserved; no part of this publication may be reproduced, stored in a retrieval system, or transmitted in any form or by any means, electronic, mechanical, photocopying, recording or otherwise without the prior written consent of the publisher or a licence permitting copying in the UK issued by the Copyright Licensing Agency Ltd. www.cla.co.uk

ISBN 978-1-78222-655-0

Book design, layout and production management by Into Print

www.intoprint.net

+44 (0)1604 832149

For

4

***"HEY!** Leave my food alone!"*

Tye takes his hidden store.
A grey squirrel grabs the food
and runs off with the hoard,
he turns around and says:

> **"The park is closing soon,
> so, no more food to hunt!"**

Then he gives a mighty grunt!

> **"HARRUMPH!
> The nuts are mine now Tye…
> you are stumped!"**

Tye looks surprised, a park he has lived in all his life is *closing*? How absurd! He angrily flicks his bushy tail.
The park trees look bleak in autumn,
the bark is flaking and stripped bare,
the summer heatwave dried them out.
The grass is patchy and soiled,
people play on the grass.

There's a notice board saying

NO BALL GAMES

Families still do what they like,
not many people donate money to care for the park, funds
are getting low, just like many play areas the
park will be sold, and soon it will go. Houses will be built on
the land or maybe a shop or two?
but the most important thing of all,
Tye will lose his home, and he doesn't know what he's going
to do.

"I will have to go and explore."

Tye needs to find a new home.

He scurries up a tree then jumps high onto another branch
and runs back down and over the pond.
He stops to see his reflection,
while resting on the ground.

"I will find a new area with lots of trees to build a new nest!"

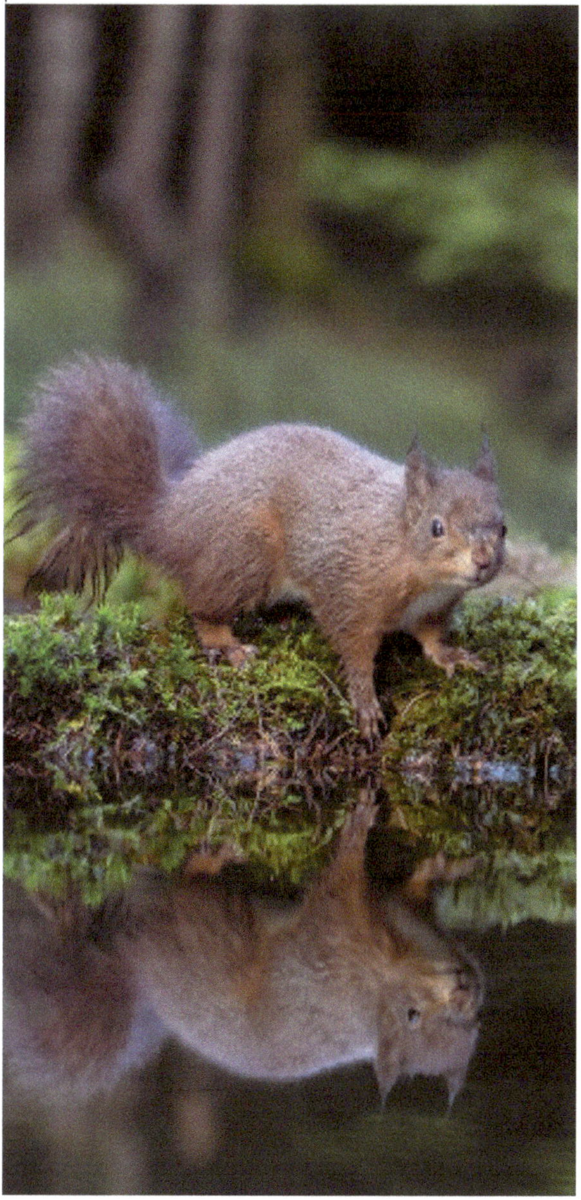

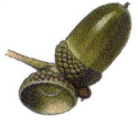

Tye is cute and cheeky, he chats happily when he's in a good mood.
He will do his best to search for a place to live to store his nut food.
He leaves the park and runs across the road going up a drain pipe onto a roof, then he jumps from house to house and notices in the distance something bright, it's a kingfisher on a tree stump, pondering about the wonders of life!

Tye scampers over the house rooftops crossing many roads, then he runs down the wall of a stone home and sits at the foot of the tree stump looking up to the kingfisher bird;
Tye says,

　"Hi! Pretty bird"

The kingfisher looks at Tye
with a questioning stare:

　"Why are you here red squirrel?"

9

She spreads her wings ready to hunt for fish swimming in a river nearby.
She glides onto a mossy branch then curiously looks down at Tye.
Tye notices an acorn on the ground. He picks it up and offers it to the colourful blue bird. The Kingfisher doesn't eat acorns, so she flies down and cheekily pecks the squirrel's red fur.

"OUCH!" squeals Tye and runs into a bush, then he peeps his head out twitching his whiskers:

"Sorry for my noisy fuss! Have you got a name kingfisher? My name is Tye."

He looks at the bird cautiously, he doesn't want to get pecked again.

"My name is Ava" the striking bird said,
then she says:

*"No acorns for me. I eat insects, fish and spiders please, I burrow a hole in the bank I don't live in the trees, so are you looking for a new home?
I am sorry for pecking you."*

She sheepishly bows her head.

Tye leaps in excitement! and peers into a deep ditch filled with rain water on the towpath that shimmers
from the autumn sun glows.
Tye likes this river area it's quieter than the park, he sees his reflection in the puddle and thinks he has a new red squirrel brother!

"WOW! This is COOL! he says with a smile, having another look at his reflection for a longer while.

"I am *cute*!"

Tye feels almighty and it shows!

Ava sings a sharp trill loudly,

"Tye! Don't let your ego grow!"

Ava flies over his head and nose dives over the ditch into the rippling river water flowing by.

She hits the water with a great big **Splosh!** and water droplets spray high! She goes down under and
rises with two fish in her beak then drops them on the ground, saying;

   "Tye do you eat fish?"

She shakes herself and flies back onto the branch. She is wet through from the fishing dip, then she puffs her feathers with a ruffle and a shuffle.

   "No! I do NOT eat fish!" says Tye loudly.

He paws a hole in the soil and hides the acorn with a noisy scuffle.
Then he gazes at Ava twitching his nose and asks;

   "*Can I stay and live here Ava?"*

Tye really hopes she will agree.

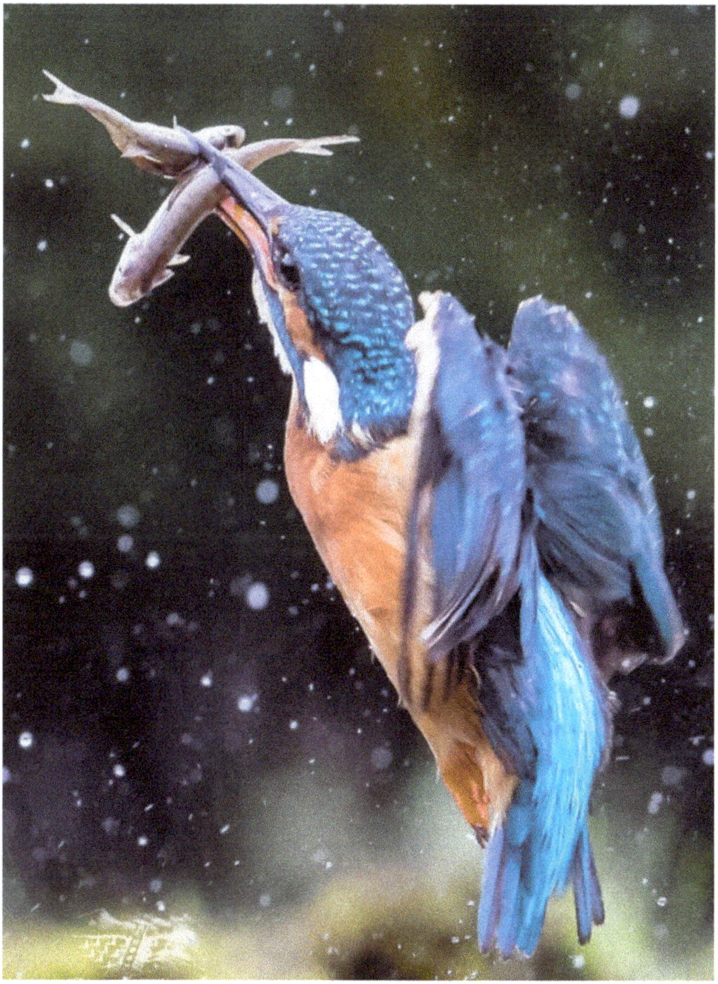

Ava flies to the fish, swallows them both, then flies back onto the mossy branch, bows her head and whispers:

"I am sorry Tye, but I have to move from this riverside."

"Why?" says Tye. "This place is great!
Much better than the park."

Tye jumps onto a mossy branch; he likes this river area with a few trees and his new bird friend. His tail sways in the cool wind breeze.
His whiskers twitch, then he scratches an itch, and snuffles as the wind blows.

Ava dives into the water again and rises with water droplets cascading in showers like tiny
bubbles ready to explode.

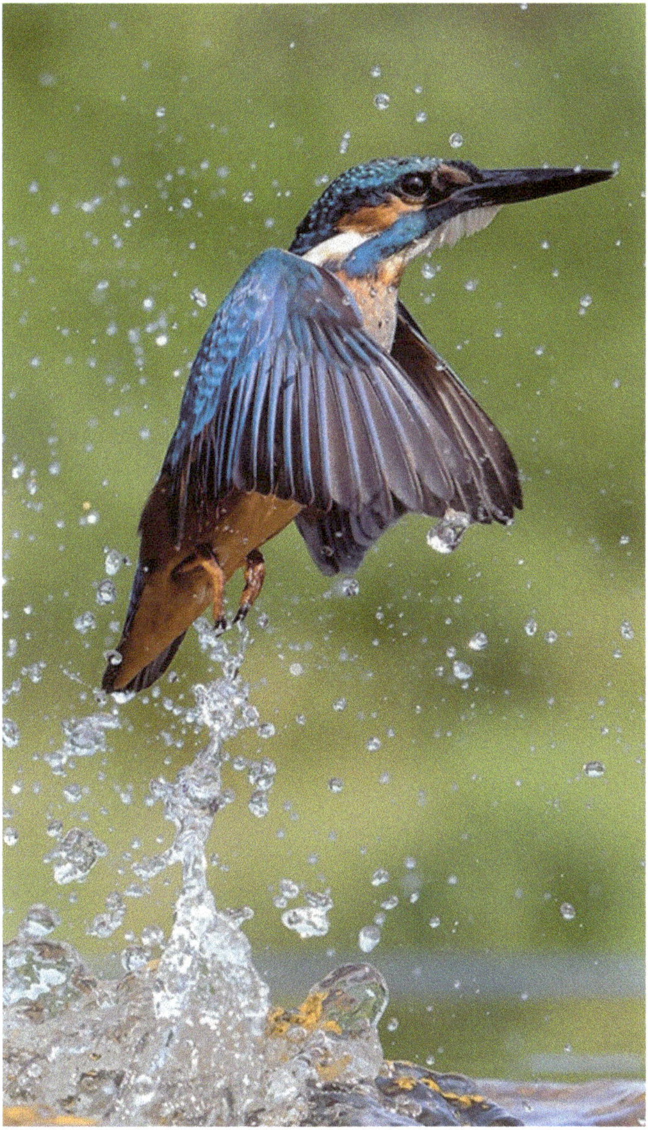

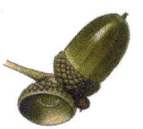

Ava kingfisher puts on a great performing show!
she explains;

> "The water is polluted Tye!
> The fish I eat die and sink to the bottom of the river bed.
> The pollution in the air is dangerous,
> I want to fly where the river is clear and clean.
> No junk in the water, no spills of bad flow, no litter and plastic bags to hurt us or buildings pulled down to make new homes.
> These actions hurt the wildlife who depend on clean air and food, not everyone is a bad human, but a lot are not very good."

Ava looks at Tye and offers a wing of friendship so Tye sits next her and she embraces him with her wing.
They stare at the river on the mossy branch and Tye knows he needs to

find a new home for 'both' of them.

Tye gives Ava a hug, and flicks his tail high, and nudges her bright orange feathered breast to say goodbye.

"Ava I will have to move on and find a place that's suitable to live in. I will come back and tell you when I have found a nice place, we will be okay."

He positively smiles and winks with a twinkle in his eye.
Ava bounces up and down happily, nodding her head. There must be somewhere
cleaner than this polluted river bed.
Ava has found a new friend in Tye and hopes he will find…
a new home.

"Good luck Tye. Stay safe, stay cheerful, and find a lovely place to rest. Thank you kind squirrel!"

Ava spreads her wings and swoops down into the water and rises feathered wet.

"That's the bath over, now I must find some food to eat again."

She waves a winged goodbye and
Tye waves back:

*"Good bye, for now Ava!
I will be back soon."*

Tye runs down a big tree trunk and scampers under a bridge wondering who else he will meet.
Then he leaps over a wall, and crosses three streets. He sees a woody area all secluded and quiet;
he jumps over the enclosure fence and enters somewhere wild.

The moonlight is dusky and spooky, the sky dimming fast, and Tye wonders if he will find nuts to eat for tea before the cold air sets in at night.

"Hey bushy tail! Get out of my wood it's private here. No squirrels allowed!"

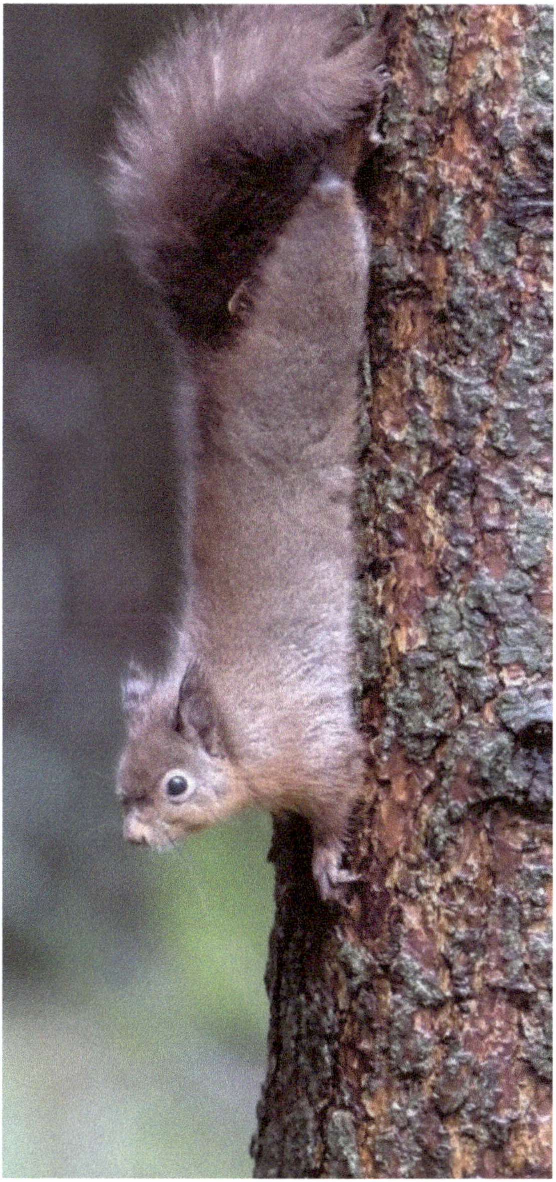

A badger appears from behind a tree looking annoyed.
Tye is surprised:

"Oh! Sorry badger, it is a little early for you to be out and about?"

Tye is wondering why the badger doesn't like squirrel visitors.
The badger grumpily answers;

*"I am digging for worms, I cannot see them very well as I have poor eyesight. My smell and hearing are stronger, that's why I go out at night.
I like acorns and insects too, but the wood is going soon, so there's not enough nuts for me or you!"*

Badger looks very disappointed.
Tye holds out his paw in friendship;

*"What is your name badger?
My name is Tye."*

"Rocco" says the badger.

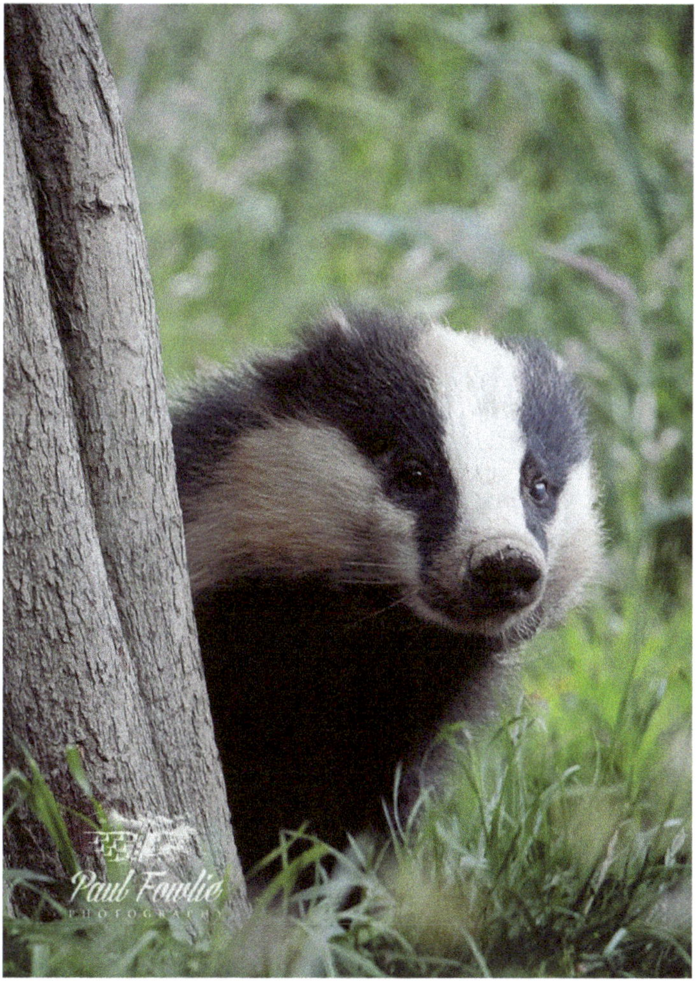
Paul Fowlie
PHOTOGRAPHY

He returns the greeting and they both touch paws and smile.

> *"I will find food for you to eat Rocco. I can find food faster than you."*

Tye wants the Badger to like him as a friend, so finding food for Rocco is a good plan. Tye scurries around and digs the earth and worms pop up, then he climbs the trees and shakes the leaves, acorns and insects fall
in a heap.

Rocco badger says;

> *"That's a huge food treat to eat!
> Thank you my new friend Tye!"*

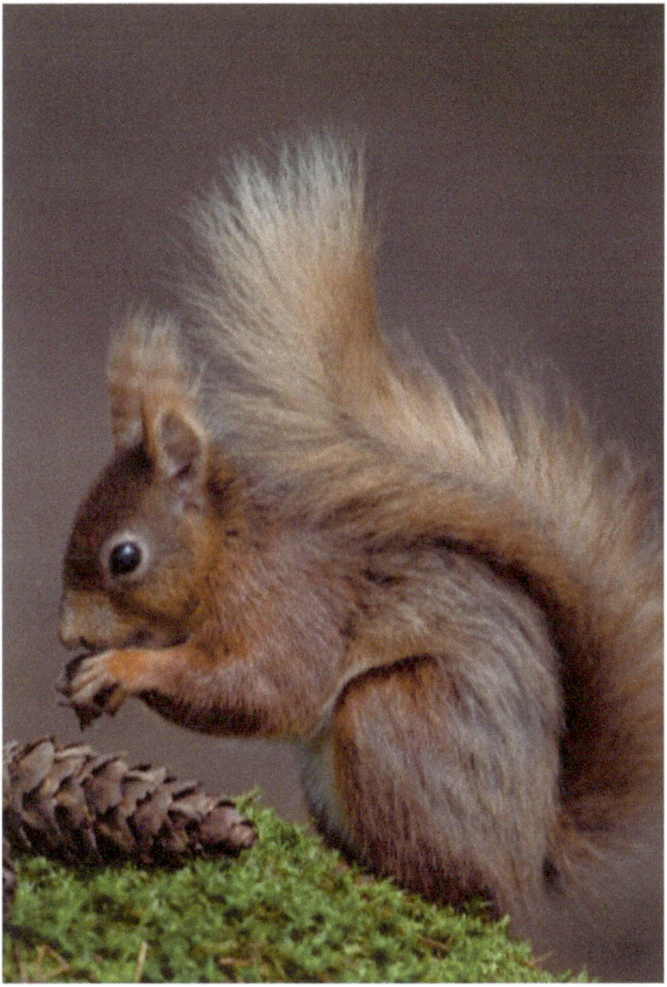

They sit down to eat together, and the sky turns a dark moody grey, the pale moon starts to awaken, as the clouds fade away.

Rocco explains to Tye that the forest is dwindling,
a few trees are left to decay and rot. Some trees are chopped for people to use in building structures and pallets to help working life move on. Some trees are recycled into paper, and furniture made from wood.

The humans seem to need more and more trees, so some woodland disappears for good.

> *"I am looking for a new home, but this woodland is not the right place"* says a disappointed Tye with a sad face.

> *"I will have to look for a new home too!"* Rocco huffs and agrees.

> *"It's not fair that animals are losing their homes through humans' comfort needs and greed."*

Tye is annoyed.

27

Rocco happily says;

> "Thank you for the food Tye, you may sleep in my sett tonight. We can have breakfast together before you look for a new habitat site."

Rocco knows that Tye is a sharing caring red squirrel.
Tye replies;

> "I will rest tonight in your cosy sett, and before I go tomorrow, I will find you more food, and then I will look for a new home to lay a nest bed!"

There must be a special place somewhere out there for all of them to share?
He hears a soft grunting sound,
Rocco is snoozing, his tummy full of insects and nut food.

> *"Goodnight Rocco"* Tye says sleepily.

It's good to make new friends, and soon Tye is grunting soft dreams next to Rocco with his tail comfortably curled around him.

The next day Tye finds Rocco some breakfast and begins his journey, his new home plans are bigger than he expected, where is he going to find a new place for them all?
He bounds through the woodland, the area is very big. Tye feels sad the trees will soon be logs and twigs.
He hears a barn owl screech
which surprises him because it's daylight and barn owls are normally asleep and hunt at night.

"Over here, over here little squirrel!"

The barn owl is roosting nearby.

He is hiding in a hole of a tree near a small hut, and a brook ripples waves over pebbles and water reeds; the brook isn't deep and looks very clean.

The owl is curious and Tye is wondering if the owl might want something to eat.

*"Hello owl, what is your name?
My name is Tye! Would you like me to help you find a mouse or a shrew?"*

Tye is happy to help to look for food, he hopes the barn owl will become his new friend, and he likes meeting someone new.

The owl stretches his wings that span out in a curve hooting excitedly:

*"**Whoo-hoo!** My name is Quinn, it's nice to meet a squirrel who is looking for a new home to live in!"*

Quinn offers his dangly claw foot to greet Tye, and Tye touches his foot with his paw, with a friendly…

"Hi!"

He breathes in deeply and
gives a very long sigh;

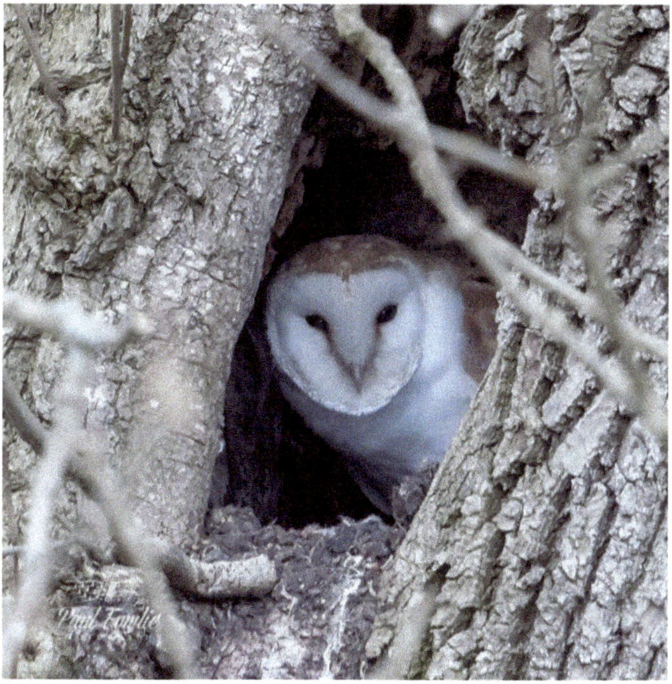

> "I need to find a new home for myself and my two friends, our habitats are disappearing in this modern way of living today."

Quinn arches his wings and flies up to a tree and pulls a pine cone off and drops it at Tye's feet.

> "There you go squirrel have a snack treat, and we will sit together to discuss what your next move will be."

The owl is very wise and calm and seems unconcerned with the ways of living, he lives for the moment but
he is still kind and giving.

> "Tye I have freedom to move and live my life the way I want, because there is always some-where to hide to make my home. I live my life by night it's quiet and more peaceful to roam, and as long as I can catch something to eat, I will always find somewhere to call home." Quinn hoots quietly.

Tye puts his paw on Quinn's smooth feathered white breast and strokes it gently.

"You look sad beautiful wise bird I sense you are lonely inside, so I welcome you as my friend and I will happily let you live with me and my friends for company if you like."

Quinn hoots in delight and flaps his wings in happiness, creating a WHOOSH of gusting air blowing fallen leaves everwhere, he shrieks:

"Tye! You are awesome! I like you a lot! but will your friends like me?" he questions curiously.

Tye springs in the air onto a fence and Quinn sits on the post. Quinn likes the friendly squirrel so much he decides to help Tye to find a new home.
Quinn can spot danger he can see from high above, and he can also see ahead and view areas of land that are quiet and clean enough to check.
Tye feels protected. It's great to find someone who cares, who will shelter him from harm and always be there.

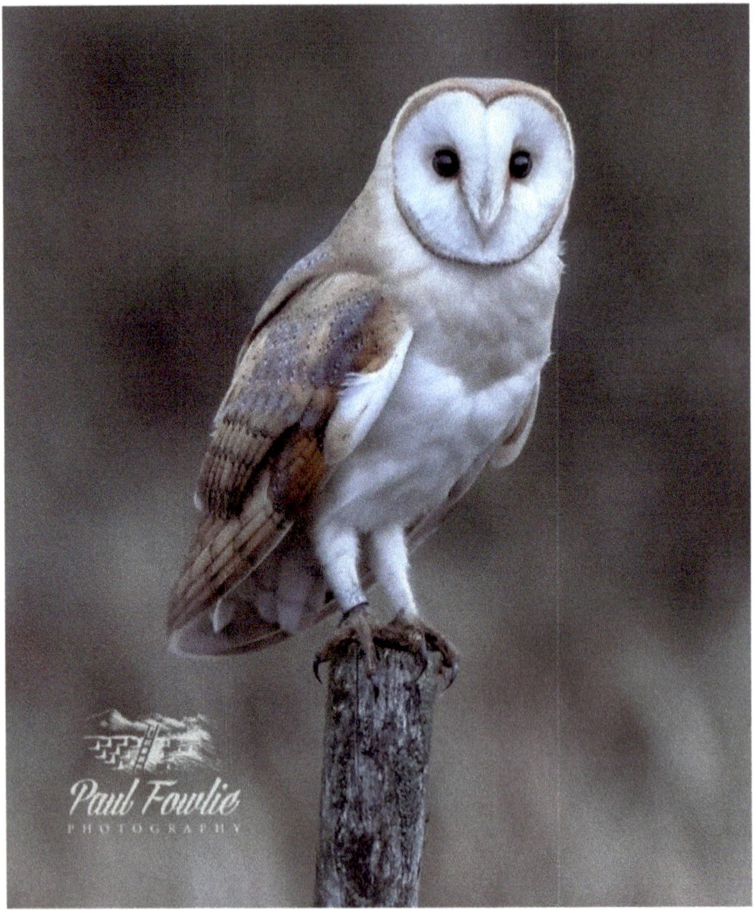
Paul Fowlie
PHOTOGRAPHY

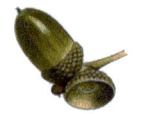

Together they leave the wood and decide to head further south where there are more open fields and less human homes about.
They cross more land that's sparse but there isn't much water there so they cannot search for food.

> "This is a shame its quiet and wild but it won't suit our kingfisher friend so we will only stay for a while."

Tye sprints up the tree that's isolated standing alone to see if there are seeds or fruit to taste, and Quinn flies to the lower branches wondering where to find a suitable place to live and rest.

After a thinking moment…

Quinn spread his wings. He flies high and soars over the woodland area and over the grassy moors.

> "Where are you going Quinn?"

Tye looks from the tree branch. Quinn looks back and waves with his wing;

> "I will be back my friend Tye,
> I'm not saying goodbye!"

Then the great wise barn owl
disappears out of view.

> "Come back soon!" Tye says.

He is hoping the barn owl finds an
area that's suitable and new.

Tye ventures on alone to the next area of land; more trees
and rocky hills but not the sort of water area that Ava will
call home.

> *"The pool area is clear but looks empty with nothing
> swimming near the surface, if the fish are hiding in the
> water, they are clever to not appear!"*

Tye is annoyed.

Tye shoots up a tree, he has plenty of choice,
then he prunes the leaves and branches making gnawing
sounds in his voice.

The branches above him begin to shake, Tye looks above …

… and someone says:

> "Hi! How are you mate?"

A pine marten looks closely at Tye, he sits on the branch with a stern eye.

> "Oh wow!" says Tye. "My cousins the grey squirrels are wary of you!"

Red and grey squirrels struggle to be friends, the greys are bullies they take their food and scare them away, and the pine marten helps the red squirrels to keep their home ground.
Tye hopes the pine marten will be his friend, he thinks he is a hero for the red squirrel family.
Any living thing can become extinct if food supplies perish, hunting wipes out, and land disappears.

> "My name is Tye! Hi! My hero,
> What is your name?"

Tye lowers his head in respect.

The pine marten laughs!

"Ok mate! Let's not be serious.

*My name is Jasper and I like to make new friends, sometimes I can be mean, but I have a good heart, and when I become a friend it's a life time friendship that will never part.
Tye you look friendly and kind so what are you doing on my side of the wood?"*

Jasper smiles a friendly glance and offers a welcoming paw touch,
to Tye as a new friend.
Tye returns the greeting and tells Jasper that Quinn is looking for a place suitable for Ava and Rocco to live. They are all creating a new habitat in the right area. Jasper says:

"Hmm! I see! Does this include me?"

Jasper lives alone he's never found a mate, so he hasn't a family to feed and look after, he quite likes the idea of living with a kingfisher, a badger, an owl and a red squirrel it sounds like fun and great company.

"Off course you can live with us Jasper!"

Tye is very pleased. If a grey squirrel tries to pinch his food store, Jasper will chase the grey squirrel away before he gets the hidden hoard.
A shadow and a breeze cast over them and Quinn lands in the tree.

"Great! you are back Quinn did you find anything?"

Tye is excited…

Quinn has a happy glint in his eye. He seems a bit uncertain about Jasper being a friend to Tye! Quinn whispers in Tye's ear.

> "Tye are you sure you can trust a pine marten as a friend, you know he might get hungry and I will never see you again?"

Quinn shelters Tye and gives him a concerned wink-wink of his eye.
Tye grins:

> "Thanks for caring Quinn. I am sure Jasper is a good soul and as long as I keep him in a good food supply, I don't think he will feel hungry as time goes by you know I like feeding you all"

Tye thinks it's cute that Quinn cares.

Quinn sits thoughtfully then flies to Jasper who has ventured to another tree to eat some berries.

"Hello new friend Jasper, I am Quinn,
I want to welcome you to our friendship group and help you
learn something."

Quinn extends his wing in greeting,
Jasper touches his wing with one paw.

"Thank you, wise barn owl Quinn,
please tell me more. I am listening."

Quinn lowers his voice to a small hoot,
and says quietly;

"Trust is very important in friendship, it really is for all,
if there's no trust from within the heart and soul,
there will be no friendships at all."

Tye leaps into the berry tree and smiles at his friends.

"Great! We are all mates now, so where is the habitat to build
our new home Quinn? I must admit I am starting to feel tired
it has been a long day hunting for a home!"

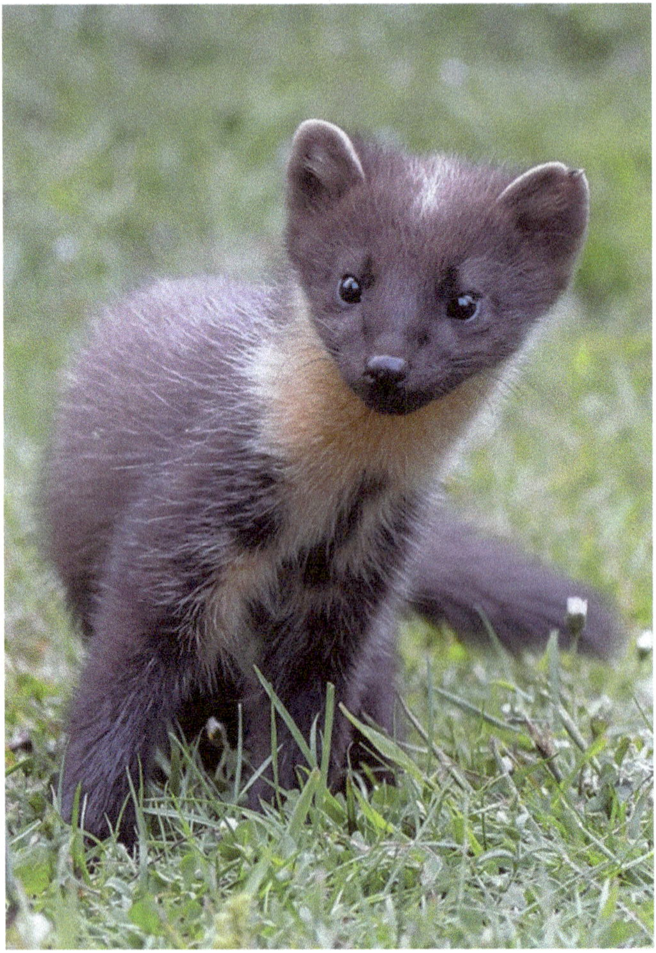

Tye yawns.
Quinn gives a knowing look,
and says quietly:

> "Tomorrow I will lead the way,
> over a brook, through two haystack fields, four villages, and then it's not far away."

Quinn is satisfied that he has found a great place for all the friends to reside.

Tye yawns again, and turns to Jasper:

> " Do you want to be part of our family Jasper?
> This woodland is not conserved,
> I don't want you to be left behind when the trees dwindle, and the animals lose their land. Humans greed for money is getting out of control, because the need to earn more makes some humans not care for animals, insects or birds at all. For every wooded land that's taken, a new one must be built close by, because when the last tree has perished, does everyone eat money? and not breathe on this earth?
>
> There are lots of areas that stay natural for creatures to breed and live, so thankfully not all humans are bad, and it's their kindness that helps creatures to exist."

Jasper listens to Tye's wise words then he springs up to a berry tree and runs down clutching some berries:

> "Here Tye please have a snack before you sleep. Of course I am coming with you, and you are so kind to help find food for all of us to eat.
> You may share my den tonight and sleep
> well until the dawn, then Quinn can lead us to the conservation area where we can live happily for ever more."

Jasper gives Tye a hug.

Tye is excited he has a new brother.

> "Before we will go to the new land, I will go and tell our sister Ava kingfisher, and our brother Rocco badger. I hope there will be plenty of water for Ava to fish, I might start liking that strange meal dish."

Tye's not really convinced but he will try new food in the future.
Quinn flies to them and hoots;

> "Yes, there is a fishing lake next to the preserved woodland, and rivers and streams nearby. There's a relic of a castle for me to roost in and so many trees in supply.

The humans have a visitor centre that shows the areas history present and past, and the humans who look after this land are passionate and caring at last.
They plant new trees and till the earth, and many do not get paid, because they are humans who love natural surroundings and want to protect all living things there."

Tye and Jasper jump in excitement!

This sounds like PARADISE!

Quinn continues with a thought for them all to sleep on;

"There are four sides to human nature, either they are greedy for lifestyles that are too grand, or they are humble and earthy to protect the natural lands,

or sadly they just don't care at all!

The fourth side has the better balance, to live life comfortably, but also to be aware and care. Every human being has a responsibility to show their concern for the environment,
to keep it clean for all creatures and plant life on earth.

*I know this place I am taking you to, because I have lived there, and I have the freedom to stay where I want to, and that's why I have gained wisdom and knowledge and view the changing world we live through.
Now I must rest so we can venture on to the safe land to settle in, I need to snooze for a short while,
goodnight Tye and Jasper."*

Quinn nods his head and settles on a post, but the animals were already nestled in Jasper's home asleep, foot to foot in a cosy den bed. Quinn tucks his beak into his chest, and hoots quietly;

"My cute little friends rest peacefully."

But he always keeps one eye open in the moonlit sky to see who is wandering by.

The sun rises the next morn with a beautiful pink and yellow sky, and Tye and Jasper awake with a yawn and open one sleepy eye. Quinn flies to Jasper's den clutching food in his clawed feet.

> *"Good morning, here's some nuts and seeds for breakfast. I don't normally fly by daylight, but I will show you the way to our new home."*

Quinn is bright and cheerful, and he managed to get a few sleep winks, while remaining on guard to protect his new friends.
Tye nibbles the food and says;

> *"I am going back to fetch Rocco and Ava so they can travel with us and see their new home today."*

Quinn thinks this is a good idea they can all see the protected land at the same time.

Tye asks Jasper:

> "Jasper are you coming with me to meet the other two in our family?
> It is important for all of us to get along."

Jasper agrees he would like to meet Rocco and Ava and accompany Tye on the journey to fetch them.
Tye and Jasper head back and Quinn decides to have a few more sleep winks until they return.

The two friends travel back and they
soon reach Rocco's home and see the badger's sett in a mess.

> "Oh no! what has happened here?
> Where's Rocco he is nowhere to be seen?"

They peer inside the sett, it looks untidy and unclean.
Tye is upset so Jasper puts his arm around his 'squirrel' brother and whispers in a quiet tone;

> "Don't worry Tye, we will find him today!"

They both look everywhere, in the bushes, behind the trees, in burrows, and couldn't see Rocco anywhere…

Then a nose peeps out from another sett that Tye didn't see, it is an old sett covered in leaves and Rocco's face appears with scratches on his head, and his fur is muddy, and he said;

> *"Tye you are back! Have you found a new home? I need to leave this place as hunters have been, they destroyed all the badgers' setts and I had to flee, this is my old home. I created a tunnel to another so when the hunters came, I burrowed to the other."*

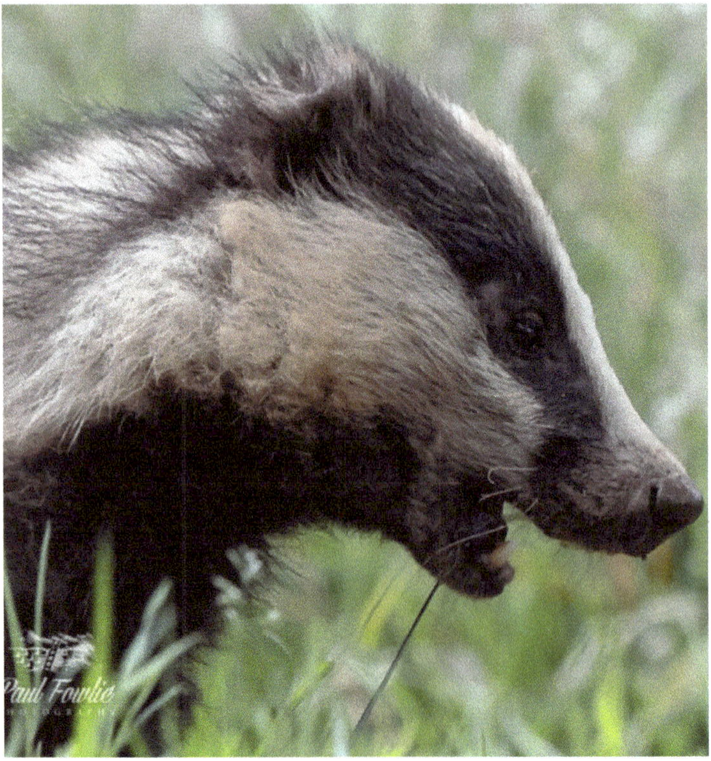
Paul Fowlie

Rocco is happy to see Tye, then he notices Jasper. He runs from his sett, and looks from behind a tree.
Rocco is annoyed, he says to Jasper;

> "Hello, are you friend or foe? because I just want a peaceful life with no fighting you know!"

Jasper looks at the badger they rarely get on, he usually keeps away from them, but he feels sorry for this one.

> "My name is Jasper and I am sad that humans came, and they are not very nice, but all I want is to be your friend and live happily together in our new protected paradise, let me clean you up? Please!"

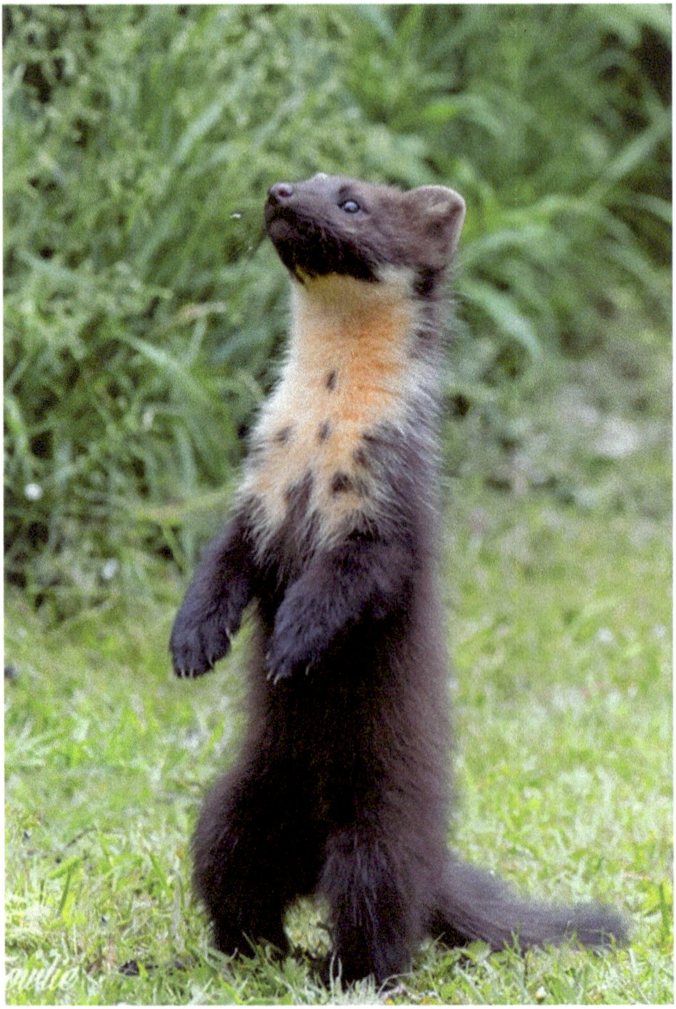

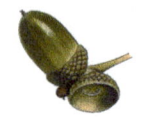

Jasper and Tye lick the mud off Rocco's fur and Rocco is glad they are family, he thanks Jasper for caring and welcomes him as a friend.
They all continue their journey to find Ava and they hope she is ok, then they spot her sitting on a mossy leaf branch with a fish in her mouth!

"Hey! Tye! you are back! Are you ready to eat fish yet?" Ava says with a wink, and then she sees Jasper. She drops the fish and speedily flies to her canal bank burrow to hide.

"My cousin eats fish! He lives near a river. I will try it Ava, thank you for my dinner!"

Jasper is hungry.
Tye flicks his tail, and shouts to Ava;

"Jasper is a friend he's not going to give you trouble. He's my brother!"

Ava looks out of her burrow;

"He looks nothing like a squirrel! but if you say you are bonded and you both see eye to eye, I will trust him as a friend my dear red squirrel friend Tye."

The four friends go back to Quinn and together they follow Quinn who flies in front to lead them to their new home.

The animals enter the conservation area and the view is beautiful, there are lots of trees and hilly steeps, and burrow holes in the ground with clusters of fern leaves everywhere.

A ruined castle is in the distance, a lake across the other side, which is bigger than Ava expected, and a brook is flowing through the vast open land. The flowing waters look fresh and clean and Ava can have a splash!

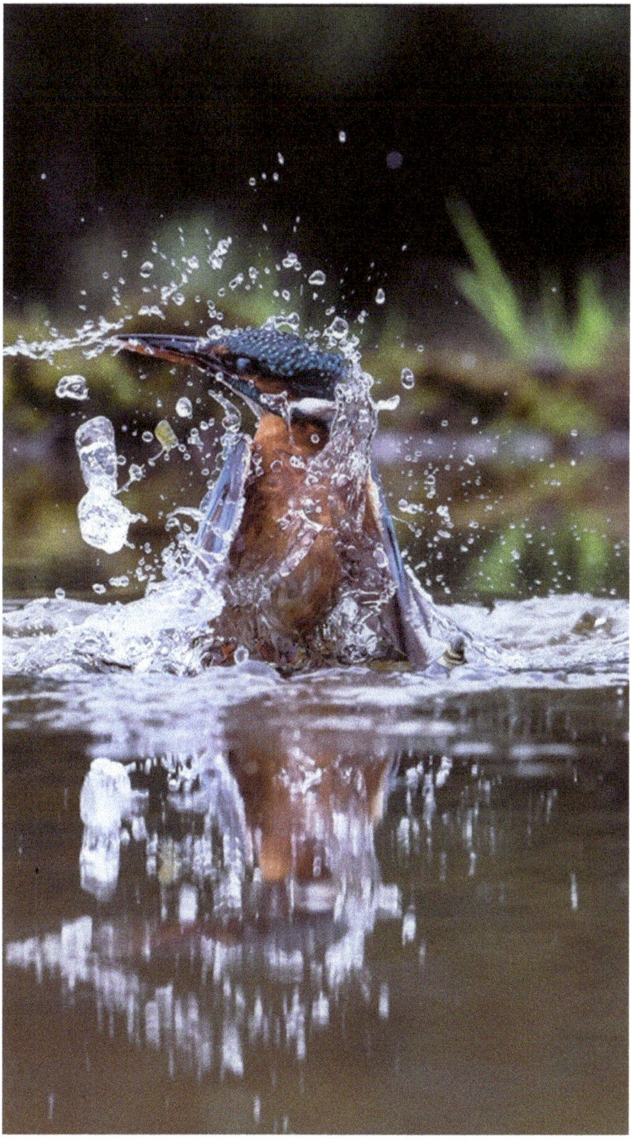

"Oh! Wow Quinn!" they all exclaim. *"It's so big!"*

They were in awe.

Quinn's friends said cheerfully;

"This is wonderful to make our new homes to rest."

Tye notices humans planting new trees and children are helping too.

He is pleased.

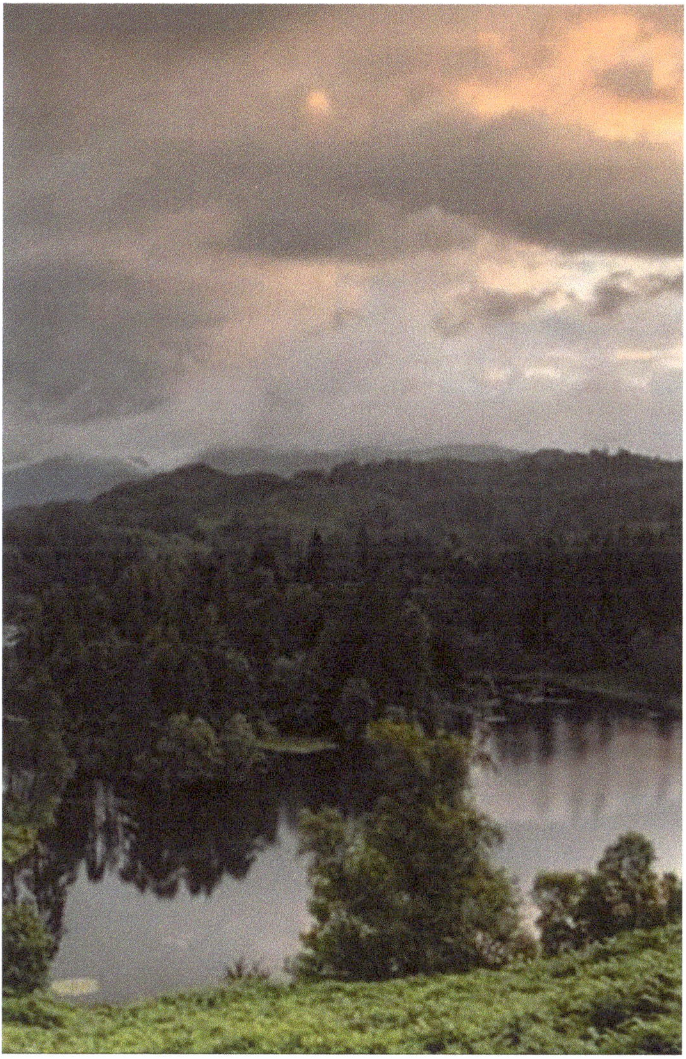

Tye says:

> "Humans are not all bad, but others do not learn, we must work together to protect this beautiful Earth.
> If more humans try to improve the environment, plant a tree, flowers and herbs, stop littering, and enjoy pretty nature places more, we will have a healthier planet for all to live in and enjoy."

The woodland friends agree with Tye.
They all form a circle and group hug together, and vow to look out for each other for ever.
Rocco, Jasper and Ava happily go off to explore their lovely surroundings.
Tye turns to Quinn and thanks him for finding their home, and Quinn hoots;

> "Young Tye, YOU are the hero!

> You decided to find a new home, but you also bond to the animals you meet, you feed them, and welcome them as family too. You show kindness and care and I already knew the land was there."

Tye and Quinn see a large stag standing nearby, and they both say with a wink of an eye:

"Hey stag would you like us to find you some food?"

The stag answers:

"Welcome! to this park new woodland friends and thank you for the offer of food. **'Kind humans'** care for us here and feed all the deer."

He blinks a
wink back, with his eye.

Kate Dobrowolska

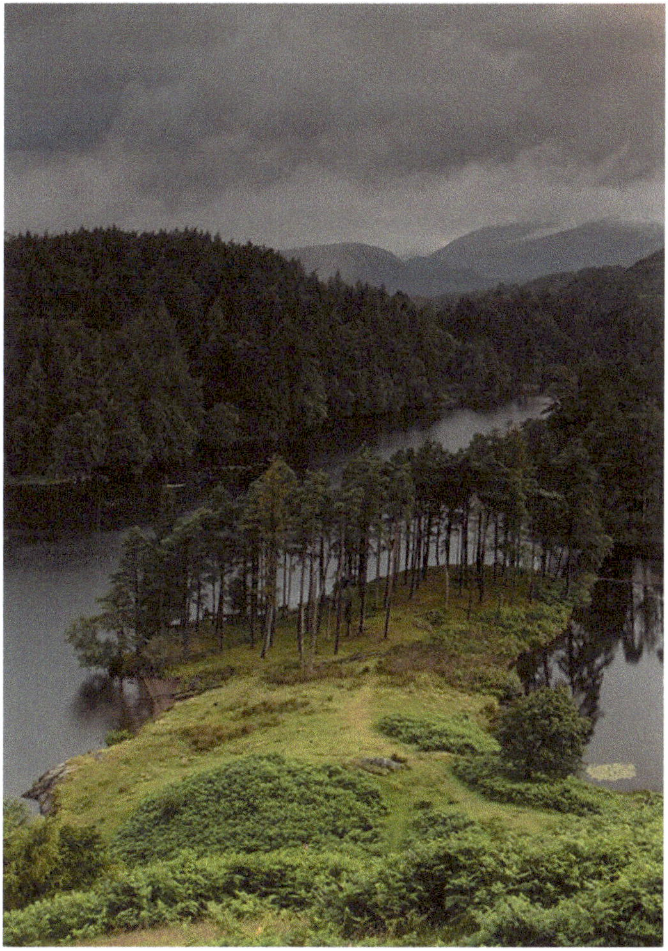

Other children's books by Kate Dobrowolska

∾

Orion and Luna Fly to the Arctic
a "Save Our Planet" story with activities, and pictures to colour in

Mira
a story of friendship and unity inspired by Polish tales

Animals Under the Weather
positive animal poems and illustrations

Animals in a Mess
quirky animal poems and illustrations

Animals in a Quandary
positive tales with illustrations, and pictures to colour in

The Adventures of Russ Crow
two crows fall out of their nest one morning and find themselves in an exciting new world of monsters and curious creatures

Chasing the New Dawn
three tales of enlightenment for young children

I grew up in an East Midland village 'Mountsorrel'.
My childhood was filled with nature walks by a canal and climbing the memorial hills; an Idyllic life, quiet, friendly and rural. I appreciated the natural beauty of the surrounding Charnwood villages, and spent weekends bike riding and visiting friends who lived there. I am privileged to show the amazing beautiful wildlife pictures photographed by
Paul Fowlie who is an International Award-winning Photographer
based in the **Yorkshire Dales**

Please keep the earth clean and protect all living things from harm.

Lightning Source UK Ltd.
Milton Keynes UK
UKHW021006080519
342309UK00006B/43/P

9 781782 226550